Congressional Research Service

Budgetary Treatment of Federal Credit (Direct Loans and Loan Guarantees): Concepts, History, and Issues for the 112th Congress

James M. Bickley
Specialist in Public Finance

July 27, 2012

Congressional Research Service

7-5700

www.crs.gov

R42632

Summary

The U.S. government uses federal credit (direct loans and loan guarantees) to allocate financial capital to a range of areas, including home ownership, higher education, small business, agriculture, and energy. At the end of FY2011, outstanding federal credit totaled $2.9 trillion. This report explains the budgetary treatment of federal credit, examines proposed reforms, and describes relevant bills introduced in the 112th Congress.

Title V of the Omnibus Budget Reconciliation Act of 1990 (P.L. 101-508), the Federal Credit Reform Act of 1990 or FCRA, changed how the unified budget reports the cost of federal credit activities (i.e., federal direct loans and loan guarantees) to an accrual basis beginning in 1992. Before FY1992, for a given fiscal year, the budgetary cost of a new direct loan or loan guarantee was the net cash flow for that fiscal year. This cash flow measure did not accurately reflect the cost of a loan or loan guarantee, which is its subsidy cost over the entire life of the loan or loan guarantee, that is, its accrual cost.

Beginning with FY1992, FCRA required that the reported budgetary cost of a credit program equal the estimated subsidy costs at the time the credit is provided. The FCRA defines the subsidy cost as "the estimated long-term cost to the government of a direct loan or a loan guarantee, calculated on a net present value basis, excluding administrative costs." This arguably places the cost of federal credit programs on a budgetary basis equivalent to other federal outlays. Because the subsidy costs of discretionary credit programs (such as the business loan programs of the Small Business Administration and the loan guarantee programs of the Export-Import Bank) are now provided through appropriations acts, this change meant that discretionary credit programs must compete with other discretionary programs on an equal basis. In contrast, funding for most mandatory credit programs (generally entitlement programs) is provided by permanent appropriations. The director of the Office of Management and Budget (OMB) is responsible for coordinating the estimation of subsidy costs to the federal government.

Since the passage of the FCRA, federal agencies, working with OMB, have steadily improved their compliance with credit reform standards. In October 1990, the Federal Accounting Standards Advisory Board (FASAB) was established. In August 1993, this board required that agencies' accounting procedures be consistent with their budgetary procedures for their federal credit programs. On August 5, 1997, the Balanced Budget Act of 1997 (P.L. 105-33) was enacted, amending the FCRA to make technical changes, including codifying several guidelines set by OMB.

Four proposals to expand credit reform have been discussed: the principles of credit reform could be applied to government-sponsored enterprises (GSEs); the principles of credit reform could be extended to federal insurance programs; the budgetary cost of capital for credit programs could be changed to include market risk; and the administrative costs of credit programs could be included in the calculation of the costs of these programs. These proposals are described in this report.

In the 112th Congress, four bills have been proposed with provisions concerning the budgetary treatment of federal credit: related bills S. 1651/H.R. 3414 (Honest Budget Act); H.R. 3581 (Budget and Accounting Transparency Act of 2011); and H.R. 3844 (Honest Budget Act of 2012). H.R. 3581 was passed by the House but has not been acted on by the Senate.

This report will be updated as issues develop and new legislation is introduced.

Contents

Tables

Appendixes

Contacts

Introduction

The U.S. government uses federal credit (direct loans and loan guarantees) to allocate capital to a range of areas including home ownership, student loans, small business, agriculture, and energy. A direct loan is "a disbursement of funds by the government to a nonfederal borrower under a contract that requires the repayment of such funds with or without interest."[1] A loan guarantee is "a pledge with respect to the payment of all or part of the principal or interest on any debt obligation of a non-federal borrower to a non-federal lender."[2] At the end of FY2011, outstanding federal direct loans totaled $838 billion and outstanding guaranteed loans totaled $2,017 billion.[3] Thus, at the end of FY2011, outstanding federal credit totaled $2.855 trillion.

The Federal Credit Reform Act of 1990 (FCRA) in the Omnibus Budget Reconciliation Act of 1990 (P.L. 101-508, §13201; 104 Stat. 1388, 1388-610) changed the budgetary treatment of federal credit from cash-flow accounting to accrual accounting. Cash flow accounting measured the cost of a new loan or new loan guarantee by its net cash flow in the fiscal year it was provided. FCRA measures the cost of new federal credit as the net present value of cash flows over the life of the loan or loan guarantee at the time the credit is extended, using Treasury interest rates to discount the value of future cash flows.[4] Some public finance experts argue that the discount rate should be changed to include market risk.

The purposes of this report are to explain the provisions of the FCRA; examine the implementation of credit reform, including credit reform provisions of the Balanced Budget Act of 1997 (P.L. 105-33, §1011; 111 Stat. 254,692); discuss proposed modifications of credit reform; and describe proposed legislation in the 112th Congress. In order to achieve these objectives, it is necessary to initially discuss justifications for credit programs, federal credit concepts, and the budgetary treatment of federal credit before the enactment of the FCRA.[5]

Before FY1992, for a given fiscal year, the reported budgetary cost of a new loan or new loan guarantee was its net cash flow for that fiscal year. This cash flow measure did not accurately reflect the cost of a loan or loan guarantee (federal credit) to the federal government, which is its subsidy cost over the entire life of the loan or loan guarantee. Using the old cash-flow method, it was often difficult for policymakers to accurately monitor and therefore make informed decisions about federal credit. In addition, administrators at agencies could understate costs by using budgetary techniques such as generating "savings" from the fees on increased volumes of new guarantees, while ignoring the increase in expected losses, and offsetting the (cash) cost of new direct loans with current year collections from old loans.

To remedy these problems, Congress included credit reform in the Omnibus Budget Reconciliation Act of 1990 (OBRA90). The President signed OBRA90 into law on November 5, 1990. The legislation added a new title to the Congressional Budget Act, Title V, the Federal

---

[1] Section 502(1) of the *Federal Credit Reform Act of 1990.*

[2] Section 502(3) of the *Federal Credit Reform Act of 1990.*

[3] U.S. Executive Office of the President, Office of Management and Budget, *Analytical Perspectives, Budget of the U.S. Government, Fiscal Year 2013* (Washington, DC: GPO, 2012), p. 401.

[4] The concepts of present value and future value are explained in examples in **Appendix A.**

[5] Some of these concepts and the budgetary treatment of federal credit before the FCRA are presented in more detail in the following source: James M. Bickley, "The Bush Administration's Proposal for Credit Reform: Background, Analysis, and Policy Issues," *Public Budgeting & Finance*, vol. 11, no. 1, spring 1991, pp. 50-65.

Credit Reform Act of 1990 (FCRA). Beginning with FY1992, the FCRA changed the methodology in the unified budget for measuring and reporting the cost of federal direct loans and federal loan guarantees.[6]

Justifications for Credit Programs

Federal credit programs are justified economically on two grounds: equity and efficiency.

Equity

Equity concerns the distributions of income, consumption, and wealth. The distribution of income has received the most emphasis among policymakers. Because economists cannot make interpersonal comparisons of utility, the optimal distributions of income, consumption, and wealth are normative; that is, they involve value judgments. In other words, economists cannot conclude that one distribution is better than another although the degree of inequality can be measured.

Another aspect of the debate on equity concerns the appropriate method of redistribution, if desired. Some Members of Congress support redistributive programs, including credit programs, to lessen income disparities. For example, credit assistance to students from lower-income families may assist the students in pursuing higher education and thus reduce income inequality. Some critics maintain that direct subsidies can usually better target assistance to the needy than can credit programs.

Efficiency

If an economy is productively *efficient*, it cannot produce more of one good without reducing the production of one or more other goods. For an economy to be efficient, private financial intermediaries should allocate capital to its most productive uses. Private financial intermediaries generally operate efficiently, but market imperfections exist, and these imperfections may cause an inadequate availability of credit in certain sectors of the economy. The Office of Management and Budget (OMB) states that market imperfections that can justify federal intervention "include information failures, monitoring problems, limited ability to secure resources, insufficient competition, externalities, and financial market instability."[7] "Education, for example, generates positive externalities because the general public benefits from the high productivity and good citizenship of a well-educated person."[8] Thus, arguably, credit assistance for higher education may improve economic efficiency.

---

[6] This report will be updated as issues develop and in the event of legislative change. For the most current information about pending legislation, please consult the Legislative Information System (LIS) at http://www.congress.gov.

[7] U.S. Executive Office of the President, Office of Management and Budget, *Analytical Perspectives, Budget of the United States Government, Fiscal Year 2013*, pp. 373-374.

[8] Ibid., p. 374.

Federal Credit Concepts

Numerous terms in financial economics have specific meanings for federal budget practices. These terms include federal credit, federal credit subsidies, and the unified budget. Some of these terms are defined in the FCRA—and are summarized in the subsequent sections.

Federal Credit

The Office of Management and Budget defines *federal credit* as federal direct loans and federal loan guarantees. The federal government extends federal credit by entering into a direct loan obligation or a loan guarantee commitment.

The FCRA defines a *direct loan* as "a disbursement of funds by the government to a nonfederal borrower under a contract that requires the repayment of such funds with or without interest" [Section 502(1)]. According to the FCRA, a *direct loan obligation* is "a binding agreement by a federal agency to make a direct loan when specified conditions are fulfilled by the borrower" [Section 502(2)]. The FCRA defines a *loan guarantee* as a "pledge with respect to the payment of all or a part of the principal or interest on any debt obligation of a non-federal borrower to a non-federal lender" [Section 502(3)]. A *loan guarantee commitment* is "a binding agreement by a federal agency to make a loan guarantee when specified conditions are fulfilled by the borrower, the lender, or any other party to the guarantee agreements" [Section 502(4)].

When either a direct loan obligation or a loan guarantee commitment is extended, the federal government determines future credit flows because the government signs a contract to provide credit. In some cases the specified conditions may not be met, and, consequently, credit will not be provided even though a contract was signed. Furthermore, there is a time lag between the signing of these contracts and the actual disbursement of a direct loan by the federal government or the actual disbursement of a guaranteed loan by a private lender. In some cases, particularly for credit for construction, credit may be disbursed by either the federal government or a private lender in increments over several fiscal years.[9]

Federal Credit Subsidies

Federal credit recipients obtain funds on more favorable terms than they could receive from the private market. OMB has described subsidies from federal direct loans as consisting of one or more of the following:

- interest rates below commercial levels,
- longer maturities than fully private loans,
- deferral of interest,
- allowance of grace periods,
- waiver or reduction of loan fees,

---

[9] For data on the estimated future cost of outstanding credit by program, see **Appendix B**. The number of credit programs depends on the degree of aggregation, and data in **Table B-1** are highly aggregated.

- higher loan amount in relation to the value of the underlying enterprise than a fully private loan, and

- availability of funds to borrowers for purposes for which the private sector would not lend—at virtually any interest rate under virtually any repayment terms.[10]

Concerning loan guarantee subsidies, OMB stated the following:

> The recipient of a federal loan guarantee receives a subsidy because the federal government covers part or all of the default risk—a subsidy conveyed by lower interest payments. Also, the federal government either levies no loan guarantee fee or charges a smaller fee than a private insurer would charge. Consequently, a private lender with a federal guarantee can charge the borrower a lower interest rate. In addition, with some guaranteed loans the federal government may pay to the lender part of the interest due on a guaranteed loan.[11]

Thus, a federal loan guarantee with or without a federal interest payment may provide a lower, equal, or higher level of subsidy than a federal direct loan.

Concept of the Unified Budget

An important budget reform that preceded credit reform was the adoption of a unified budget. Before 1967, the federal government most frequently used an administrative budget, which was not comprehensive in coverage because it excluded the trust funds (for example, the Social Security trust fund). The federal government also used two other broad budgets: the consolidated cash budget and the national income accounts budget. Each of these three budgets had a different coverage of federal programs and a different accounting method; consequently each had a different surplus or deficit.[12] Each of these budgets had weaknesses, and the simultaneous use of three different budget concepts caused confusion.[13] An important budget reform that preceded credit reform was the adoption of a unified budget.

In March 1967, the President's Commission on Budget Concepts was created and instructed to make "a thorough and objective review of budgetary concepts."[14] In October 1967, the commission produced a comprehensive report with detailed recommendations on implementing a unified budget. In its report, the commission stated that the two basic functions of the federal budget are resource allocation and macroeconomic stabilization.[15] For resource allocation, the commission believed that the budget should "provide the integrated framework for information and analyses from which the best possible choices can be made in allocating the public's money among competing claims."[16] This function of resource allocation should include comparisons

---

[10]This list of subsidies is paraphrased from the following source, U.S. Executive Office of the President, Office of Management and Budget, *Special Analysis F, Federal Credit Programs, Budget of the United States Government, Fiscal Year 1988* (Washington, DC: GPO, 1987), p. F32.

[11] Ibid., p. F33.

[12] For an explanation of these budget concepts, see *Report of the President's Commission on Budget Concepts* (Washington, DC: GPO, 1967), pp. 82-83.

[13] Ibid., p. 1.

[14] Ibid., p. 105.

[15] Ibid., p. 14.

[16] Ibid., p. 16.

among government programs and between the public and private sectors.[17] For macroeconomic stabilization, the commission maintained that the budget should contain detailed and accurate information in order to evaluate the effects of federal fiscal activities.

Furthermore, the commission stated that the budget should include data necessary to undertake discretionary countercyclical fiscal policy.[18] Thus, the commission recommended a unified budget that would be composed of all federal activities, including the trust funds and federal credit activities. The commission recommended that federal credit programs be measured by their cash flows, although it realized that this procedure provided a poor measure of the economic and budgetary effects of federal credit. In the FY1969 budget, the Johnson Administration adopted the unified budget concept, but with some structural differences from the proposal of the commission. The Johnson Administration essentially adopted commission recommendations of measuring credit by its cash flows.

Subsequent implementation of federal credit reform would improve the use of the unified budget for resource allocation and macroeconomic stabilization as originally desired by the commission.[19]

Federal Credit Reform Act of 1990

Some budget experts and policymakers criticized the cash flow treatment of federal credit in the unified budget as not accurately measuring the cost of federal credit and its effect on resource allocation. Beginning in 1983, proposals for using accrual accounting for federal credit were debated and culminated in the Federal Credit Reform Act of 1990, which is the basis for the treatment of federal credit today.[20]

The four stated purposes of the FCRA were listed in Section 501:

> (1) measure more accurately the costs of federal credit programs;

> (2) place the cost of credit programs on a budgetary basis equivalent to other federal spending;

> (3) encourage the delivery of benefits in the form most appropriate to the needs of beneficiaries; and

> (4) improve the allocation of resources among credit programs and other spending.

Subsidy Costs

The FCRA never uses the word subsidy; nevertheless, the budgetary and economic cost of a federal credit program is arguably the subsidy value at the time credit is provided. The FCRA

---

[17] Ibid.

[18] Ibid., p. 18.

[19] The budgetary treatment of federal credit before FY1992 is described in **Appendix C**.

[20] For hypothetical examples of the operation of a direct loan program and a loan guarantee program under the Federal Credit Reform Act of 1990, see **Appendix D** and **Appendix E**.

---

defines [subsidy] cost as "the estimated long-term cost to the government of a direct loan or loan guarantee, calculated on net present value basis, excluding administrative costs and any incidental effects on governmental receipts or outlays" [Section 502(5A)]. The discount rate used to calculate subsidy costs in terms of present value is the "average interest rate on marketable Treasury securities of similar maturity" [Section 502(5E)].[21] Hence, the subsidy cost of a program is determined by the amount of credit provided and the discount rate used to calculate the net present value of that credit.

Any government action that changes the estimated present value of an outstanding federal credit program is counted in the budget in the year in which the change occurs as a change in the subsidy cost of that program [Section 502(5D)]. For example, the federal government could partially forgive the repayment of principal for low-income borrowers from a particular credit program, which would increase the subsidy cost of the program.

Estimation of Subsidies

The director of the Office of Management and Budget is responsible for coordinating the estimation of subsidy costs. "The Director may delegate to agencies authority to make estimates of costs" [Section 503(a)]. But agencies must use written guidelines from the director, which are developed after consultation with the director of the Congressional Budget Office. The director of OMB and the director of CBO are responsible for developing more accurate historical data on credit programs, which are used to estimate subsidy costs (Section 503). The President's budget includes "the planned level of new direct loan obligations and new loan guarantee commitments associated with each appropriations request" (Section 504).

Budgetary Treatment

Beginning with FY1992, an appropriation for the annual subsidy cost of each credit program is made into a budget account called a *credit program account*. The subsidy cost of federal credit is scored as an outlay in the fiscal year in which the credit is disbursed by either the federal government or a private lender [Section 504(d)].

Discretionary programs providing new direct loan obligations and new loan guarantee commitments require appropriations of budget authority equal to their estimated subsidy costs. Funding for the subsidy costs of discretionary credit programs is provided in appropriation acts and must compete with other discretionary programs for funding available under the constraints of a budget resolution.

Mandatory programs, generally credit entitlements (for example, guaranteed student loans), and existing credit programs of the Commodity Credit Corporation have indefinite budget authority [Section 505(a-c)]. Most mandatory credit programs receive automatic funding for the amount of credit needed to meet the estimated demand by beneficiaries, which depends on eligibility and benefits rules contained in substantive law. For mandatory credit programs, any additional cost from reestimates of subsidies for a credit program is covered by permanent indefinite budget authority. This additional cost is displayed in a subaccount in the credit program account.

---

[21] The derivation of the discount rate was revised by the Balanced Budget Act of 1997.

Also, beginning with FY1992, each credit program has a nonbudget *financing account*. Each of these nonbudget financing accounts receives payments from its associated credit program account equal to the subsidy cost at the time a new loan or loan guarantee is provided. The financing account for each new direct loan also acquires the value of the unsubsidized portion of that loan (actual disbursements by the government minus the subsidy cost). This amount is borrowed from the Treasury through the loan program.[22]

Furthermore, the financing accounts contain all other cash flows between the public and the government associated with each credit program [Section 502(5E6-7)]. These flows include "the disbursement and repayment of loans, the payment of default losses on guarantees, and the collection of interest and fees."[23] Because they are nonbudget, the cash flows into and out of these accounts are not reflected in total outlay, receipts, or surplus/deficit. The budget authority of a credit program provides the means for the credit program account to pay to the financing account an amount equal to that program's estimated subsidy costs. The off-budget borrowing from the Treasury for the unsubsidized portion of a direct loan program is included in the national debt.

Another special account, the *liquidating account*, includes all ongoing cash flows of each credit program resulting from credit advanced prior to October 1, 1991 [Section 502(5E8)]. However, the budgetary procedures under the FCRA would apply to modifications made by the U.S. government to credit terms on credit provided before FY1992.[24]

The FCRA does not apply to the credit activities of the Federal Deposit Insurance Corporation, the National Credit Union Administration, the Resolution Trust Corporation, national flood insurance, the National Insurance Development Fund, crop insurance, or the Tennessee Valley Authority (Section 506).

Implementation

Federal Agencies

The Federal Credit Reform Act of 1990 was brief as a policy statement; it covered only five and one-half pages of the *U.S. Code, Congressional and Administrative News*.[25] Numerous details necessary to make the act operational were absent. Furthermore, many federal agencies had inadequate financial and accounting systems to implement credit reform.[26]

---

[22] These transfers within the government represent transfers of budgetary resources rather than actual financial resources.

[23] U.S. Executive Office of the President, Office of Management and Budget, *Analytical Perspectives, Budget of the United States Government, Fiscal Year 2009* (Washington, DC: GPO,2008), p. 359.

[24] U.S. Executive Office of the President, Office of Management and Budget, *The Budget System and Concepts, Budget of the United States Government, Fiscal Year 2003* (Washington, DC: GPO, 2002), p. 15.

[25] *U.S. Code, Congressional and Administrative News,* 101st Cong., 2nd sess., vol. 6 (St. Paul, MN: West Publishing Co., 1991), pp. 610-615.

[26] David B. Pariser, "Implementing Federal Credit Reform: Challenges Facing Public Sector Financial Manager," *Public Budgeting & Finance*, vol. 12, no. 4, winter 1992, p. 28.

On July 2, 1992, OMB issued a revised circular, which improved and clarified instructions for credit budget formulation.[27] Furthermore, OMB simplified its credit subsidy model to help agencies to estimate direct loan and loan guarantee subsidies.[28] In November 2000, OMB updated Circular A-129 concerning the budgetary treatment of federal credit programs.[29] On November 2, 2005, OMB also revised Circular A-11 to include federal credit reform procedures. In Circular A-11, OMB explains how agencies should fill out credit schedules in preparing their budget requests.[30] Federal agencies working with OMB have steadily improved their compliance with credit reform standards.

Since the passage of the FCRA, OMB has continued to assist agencies in upgrading the quality of subsidy estimates. Beginning with FY1994, agencies have recorded reestimates of the cost of their credit programs, and aggregate subsidy estimates have been adjusted upward or downward annually.[31] The FCRA provided for permanent indefinite authority to cover the cost of reestimates so that new appropriations would not be needed. Agencies are required to incorporate improved knowledge into their subsidy estimates for future direct loan obligations and loan guarantee commitments.[32]

The Government Accountability Office examined subsidy estimates for 10 credit programs in five agencies for the period of fiscal years 1992 through 1998. GAO found problems with supporting documentation for subsidy estimates and the reliability of subsidy rate estimates and reestimates in each agency.[33] But GAO concluded that agencies showed improvement in documenting their estimates.[34]

CBO examined credit subsidy re-estimates for the period of FY1993 through FY1999. CBO concluded that

> Projecting the losses and costs from federal credit assistance is difficult, and errors are inevitable. Although various incentives may exist for agencies to underestimate credit subsidies, the Congressional Budget Office's analysis of corrected reestimates does not reveal any pattern of bias in initial subsidy estimates. However, another problem was uncovered: the reestimates reported in the president's budget are in such disorder that analysts cannot rely on them. A few modest changes in current practice could reduce agencies' errors in preparing, reporting, and accounting for estimates and reestimates.[35]

---

[27] U.S. Executive Office of the President, Office of Management and Budget, *Budget of the United States Government, Fiscal Year 1994* (Washington, DC: GPO, 1993), p. 49.

[28] Ibid.

[29] U.S. Executive Office of the President. Office of Management and Budget, *Policies for Federal Credit Programs and Non-Tax Receivables*, Circular A-129 (Washington, DC: continually updated), p. 27.

[30] OMB's Circulars A-11 and A-129 are available at http://www.whitehouse.gov/omb/circulars.

[31] U.S. Executive Office of the President, Office of Management and Budget, *Analytical Perspectives, Budget of the United States Government, Fiscal Year 2004* (Washington, DC: GPO, 2003), p. 217; and *Analytical Perspectives, Budget of the United States Government, Fiscal Year 2009*, p. 96.

[32] U.S. Executive Office of the President, Office of Management and Budget, *Federal Credit Supplement, Budget of the United States Government, Fiscal Year 1997* (Washington, DC: GPO, 1996), pp. 48-49.

[33] U.S. General Accounting Office, *Credit Reform Greater Effort Needed to Overcome Persistent Cost Estimation Problems*, Report no. AIMD-98-14 (Washington, DC: GPO, March 1998), pp. 9-10.

[34] Ibid., p. 11.

[35] David Torregrosa, "Credit Subsidy Reestimates, 1993-99," *Public Budgeting & Finance*, vol. 21, no. 2, summer 2001, p. 114. At the time this article was published, the author was an analyst in CBO's Microeconomic and Financial (continued...)

OMB established on-budget *receipt accounts* to receive payments of earnings from the financing accounts in those cases where federal credit programs are estimated to produce net income, that is, have negative subsidies.[36] Usually, payments into a program's receipt account are recorded in the Treasury's general fund as offsetting receipts.[37] "In a few cases, the receipts are earmarked in a special fund established for the program and are available for appropriation for the program."[38]

Federal Accounting Standards Advisory Board

In October 1990, the Federal Accounting Standards Advisory Board (FASAB or "the Board") was established by the Secretary of the Treasury, the director of OMB, and the Comptroller General to consider and recommend accounting principles for the federal government. On September 15, 1992, the board issued an exposure draft recommending accounting standards for federal credit programs on a basis consistent with credit reform. The board received numerous substantive comments that were considered in revising its exposure draft, and on August 23, 1993, OMB issued the board's revised report titled *Accounting for Direct Loans and Loan Guarantees*.[39] This report provided extensive detail, including numerous arithmetic examples, clarifying credit reform practices.[40] It further required that federal agencies use of present value accounting for federal credit programs be consistent with the Federal Credit Reform Act of 1990.[41] Thus, for their credit programs, agencies' accounting procedures were now required to be consistent with their budgetary procedures.

Balanced Budget Act of 1997

On August 5, 1997, the Balanced Budget Act of 1997 was enacted. This law amended the Federal Credit Reform Act of 1990 to make some technical changes including codifying several OMB guidelines. The law made important changes that continue to govern federal credit today:

First, agencies are required to use the same discount rate to calculate the subsidy when they obligate budget authority for direct loans and loan guarantees and when submitting the agency's budget justification for the President's budget.[42] Thus, the dollar value of loans for a specific credit program is known when Congress considers subsidy appropriations for that program. Prior

---

(...continued)

Studies Division.

[36] Marvin Phaup, "Credit Reform, Negative Subsidies, and FHA," *Public Budgeting & Finance*, vol. 16, no. 1, spring 1996, p. 24.

[37] U.S. Executive Office of the President, Office of Management and Budget, *Analytical Perspectives, Budget of the United States Government, Fiscal Year 2007* (Washington, DC, GPO, 2006), p. 390.

[38] Ibid.

[39] For a discussion of the board's conclusions on issues raised by these comments, see U.S. Executive Office of the President, Office of Management and Budget, *Accounting for Direct Loans and Loan Guarantees Statement of the Federal Financial Accounting Standards*, no. 2 (Washington, DC: August 23, 1993), pp. 21-42.

[40] For a detailed example of the estimation of credit subsidies, see U.S. General Accounting Office, *Credit Subsidy Estimates for the Sections 7(a) and 504 Business Loan Programs*, Report no. T-RCED-97-197 (Washington, DC: GPO, July 16, 1997), p. 19.

[41] U.S. Executive Office of the President, Office of Management and Budget, *Accounting for Direct Loans and Loan Guarantees Statement of the Federal Financial Accounting Standards*, pp. 21-42.

[42] U.S. Executive Office of the President, Office of Management and Budget, *Analytical Perspectives, Budget of the United States, Fiscal Year 1999* (Washington, DC: GPO, 1998), p. 170.

---

to this change, agencies had used interest rates from the preceding calendar quarter to calculate the subsidy at the time a direct loan was advanced or a loan guarantee was obligated.[43]

Second, agencies are required to use the same forecast assumptions (for example, default and recovery rates) to calculate subsidy rates when they obligate credit and when preparing the President's budget.[44]

Third, agencies are required to transfer end-of-year unobligated balances in liquidating accounts (revolving funds for direct loans and loan guarantees made prior to the effective date of the FCRA) to the general fund as soon as practicable after the close of the fiscal year.[45]

Fourth, the same interest rate must be used on financing account debt (which generates interest payments to the Treasury), financing account balances, and the discount rate used to calculate subsidy costs.[46]

Fifth, the definition of the term "cost" was modified so that the discount rate is based on the timing of cash flows instead of on the term of the loan. Under this new approach, in the President's budget, a series of different rates would be used to calculate the present value of cost flows over a multi-year period. For example, for a 10-year direct loan (or loan guarantee), costs in the first year would be discounted using the interest rate on a one-year Treasury bill, costs in the second year would be discounted using the interest rate on a two-year Treasury note, etc. Under the prior approach, the interest rate of a 10-year Treasury note would have been used as the discount rate. The earlier method proved to be inferior because the flow of semiannual interest payments and the repayment of full principal on the last payment date did not match up well with yearly cost flows.[47]

Possible Payment of Subsidy Costs by Recipients

Rather than having the federal government pay for the subsidy costs of credit programs, a credit program may result in some cases in the subsidy costs being paid by credit recipients. For example, the Energy Policy Act of 2005 (P.L. 109-58; 119 Stat. 594) includes Title XVII—Incentives for Innovative Technologies. Section 1702 (b) states that

> No [loan] guarantee shall be made unless—(1) an appropriation for the cost has been made; or (2) the Secretary [of Energy] has received from the borrower a payment in full for the cost of the obligation and deposited the payment into the Treasury.

If credit recipients pay the subsidy costs and there is no ceiling on appropriations, then hypothetically there would be no limit to the size of the loan guarantee program. But this law does not state anything about an appropriations ceiling on the volume of loan guarantees. Some observers argue that loan guarantees with the recipients paying the estimated costs should not be

---

[43] Ibid.

[44] Ibid.

[45] Ibid.

[46] Ibid.

[47] U.S. Congress, Conference Committee, *Balanced Budget Act of 1997, Conference Report to Accompany H.R. 2015*, H.Rept. 105-217, 105th Cong., 1st sess. (Washington, DC: July 30, 1997), pp. 996-997.

---

provided unless there is a cap on appropriations in order to control the size of a credit program.[48] No loan guarantees for innovative fuel technology have been made in which the credit recipient has paid the estimated subsidy cost upfront.

Federal Credit in the President's FY2013 Budget

In the Federal Credit Supplement for the FY2013 budget, OMB presents the loan characteristic variables for each credit program, which are loan maturity period, borrower interest rate, grace period, upfront fees, annual fees, other fees, assumed default rate, rate of recovery on defaults, and percent of loan guaranteed (for loan guarantee programs only).[49] In addition, OMB breaks down estimated subsidy rates into four components: defaults (net of recoveries), interest, fees, and all other.[50]

For FY2013, OMB estimates an aggregate proposed subsidy budget authority of *new direct loans* of negative $33.352 billion.[51] This high negative subsidy budget authority amount was due, almost exclusively, to negative proposed subsidy budget authority of new direct loans for the Department of Education's Federal Direct Student Loan Program (negative $33.475 billion).[52] This high negative subsidy level was due primarily to the use of Treasury interest rates to discount future credit flows. Fair value budgeting, an alternative method of discounting future credit flows, is discussed in the next section.

For FY2013, OMB estimates an aggregate proposed subsidy budget authority of *new loan guarantees* of negative $9.467 billion.[53] This high negative subsidy budget authority amount was due primarily to negative proposed subsidy budget authority of new loan guarantees for the FHA-Mutual Mortgage Insurance Program Account[54] of negative $8.188 billion.[55]

Proposals for the Expansion of Reforms

Four major proposals to expand credit reform have been discussed in recent years. Some of these proposed expansions are also included in legislation described in the next section on proposed legislation in the 112th Congress.

---

[48] For a comprehensive analysis of this issue, see U.S. Government Accountability Office, *DOE Loan Guarantee Program for Projects That Employ Innovative Technologies*, Report no. GAO-07-339R, February 28, 2007.

[49] U.S. Executive Office of the President, Office of Management and Budget, *Federal Credit Supplement, Budget of the United States Government, Fiscal Year 2013*, pp. 9, 13.

[50] Ibid.

[51] U.S. Executive Office of the President, Office of Management and Budget, *Analytical Perspectives, Budget of the United States Government, Fiscal Year 2013*, pp. 405-406.

[52] Ibid., p. 405. For data on proposed loan levels on each direct loan program, see **Appendix F**.

[53] Ibid., p. 407.

[54] For an overview of FHA loans, see CRS Report RS20530, *FHA-Insured Home Loans An Overview*, by Katie Jones.

[55] Ibid., For data on proposed loan levels on each loan guarantee program, see **Appendix G**.

Inclusion of Government-Sponsored Enterprises

The principles of credit reform could be applied to government-sponsored enterprises (GSEs). GSEs are privately owned financial intermediaries, which were established and chartered by the federal government. GSEs pay lower interest rates on their securities because investors generally believe that securities issued by GSEs have an implied federal guarantee, making them appear less risky than other private sector securities.

Proponents of extending credit reform principles to GSEs have argued that the federal government has already "bailed out" one GSE (the Farm Credit System). In the late 1970s, agricultural prices declined, farm income plummeted, and agricultural land prices fell.[56] Consequently, many farmers were unable to repay their loans and the Farm Credit System incurred large losses. A series of federal efforts to assist the Farm Credit System were unsuccessful, and eventually lead to the enactment of the Agriculture Credit Act of 1987 (P.L. 100-233) on January 6, 1988.[57] This act provided federal financial assistance to prevent the Farm Credit System from defaulting on its debt. Two decades later, on September 7, 2008, the federal government placed in conservatorship or receivership two financially troubled housing GSEs: the Federal National Mortgage Association (Fannie Mae) and the Federal Home Loan Mortgage Corporation (Freddie Mac).[58] Legislation has been proposed to reform these housing enterprises.[59] Hence, proponents argue that credit reform should cover the subsidy costs to taxpayers of all GSEs.

Opponents have argued that the subsidy costs of GSEs are difficult to quantify; furthermore, the federal government has no legal responsibility to "bail out" GSEs. Opponents also maintain that the current low Treasury interest rates and the exclusion of both administrative costs and risk premiums may result in negative subsidy costs for GSEs.

Extension to Federal Insurance

The principles of credit reform could be extended to federal insurance, which is treated primarily on a cash flow basis.[60] Most federal insurance consists of deposit insurance or pension insurance.[61] The Government Accountability Office maintains that credit reform could improve the budgetary information and incentives for federal insurance.[62] But, for some federal insurance programs, significant difficulties exist in accurately estimating future claims for losses. Often, historical data are unavailable, frequent program modifications occur, and fundamental changes

---

[56] Julie Andersen Hill, "Bailouts and Credit Cycles: Fannie, Freddie, and the Farm Credit System," *Wisconsin Law Review*, vol. 2010, no. 1, July 2010, pp. 36-37.

[57] Ibid., pp. 38-42.

[58] CRS Report RS22950, *Fannie Mae and Freddie Mac in Conservatorship*, by Mark Jickling, p. 2.

[59] CRS Report R41822, *Proposals to Reform Fannie Mae and Freddie Mac in the 112th Congress*, by N. Eric Weiss.

[60] For a comprehensive analysis of the current budgetary treatment of a federal insurance program, see Congressional Budget Office, *The Budgetary Treatment of Subsidies in the National Flood Insurance Program*, Testimony of Donald B. Marron, Acting Director, before the Senate Committee on Banking, Housing, and Urban Affairs, January 25, 2006.

[61] U.S. General Accounting Office, *Budget Issues Budgeting for Federal Insurance Programs*, Report no. AIMD-97-16 (Washington, DC: September 1997), p. 6.

[62] Ibid., p. 7.

take place in the activities insured.[63] Many federal insurance programs cover types of risk that the private sector has either refused or been unable to cover.[64]

> The complexity of the issues involved and the need to build agency capacity to generate such estimates suggest that it is not feasible to integrate accrual-based costs directly into the budget at this time.[65]

GAO has suggested that a supplemental approach should precede the full inclusion of insurance programs under credit reform. Thus, GAO has recommended that accrual-based cost measures be initially included along with cash-based estimates as supplemental information in the budget documents.[66]

On April 25, 2002, GAO's director of federal budget analysis gave the following testimony before the House Committee on the budget:

> While there are significant estimation and implementation challenges, accrual-based budgeting has the potential to improve budgetary information and incentives for these programs by providing more accurate and timely recognition of the government's costs and improving the information and incentives for managing insurance costs.
>
> In 1997 we reported that the current cash-based budget generally provides incomplete information on the costs of federal insurance programs. The ultimate costs to the federal government may not be apparent up front because of time lags between the extension of the insurance, the receipt of premiums, and the payment of claims.[67]

Some opponents of the inclusion of insurance programs maintain that, because the current subsidy measure excludes administrative costs and a risk premium, some major insurance programs would record negative subsidies.

Inclusion of Market Risk

The budgetary cost to taxpayers of providing federal credit could be changed to include market risk.[68] When credit reform was debated, the Government Accountability Office (GAO), the Congressional Budget Office (CBO), the Office of Management and Budget (OMB), and the Senate Budget Committee all recommended that federal credit be measured by the net present value of credit subsidies.[69] But, GAO and the Senate Budget Committee recommended a cost-to-

---

[63] U.S. General Accounting Office, *Budget Issues Budgeting for Federal Insurance Programs*, Testimony before the Budget Task Force, Committee on the Budget, House of Representatives, Report no. T-AIMD-98-147 (Washington, DC, April 23, 1998), p. 9.

[64] Ibid.

[65] Ibid., p. 13.

[66] U.S. General Accounting Office, *Budget Issues Budgeting for Federal Insurance Programs*, Report no. AIMD-97-16, p. 10.

[67] U.S,. General Accounting Office, *Budget Process Extending Budget Controls*, Testimony of Susan J. Irving, Director, Federal Budget Analysis, before the House Committee on the Budget, April 26, 2002, p. 16.

[68] This change would require new legislation because the FCRA specifies that the subsidy cost of federal credit is the cost to the taxpayer rather than the market value to the recipient.

[69] U.S. General Accounting Office, *Budgetary Treatment of Federal Credit Programs*, Report No. AFMD-89-42 (Washington, DC, April 1989), p. 28.

the-government measure be used while CBO and OMB supported a "market-valuation oriented measurement approach, which calculates the economic benefit borrowers receive as a result of obtaining federal, rather than private sector, loans."[70]

Currently, the FCRA requires the discounting of expected cash flows at the interest rate on Treasury securities (the rate at which the government borrows money). CBO's report on federal credit subsidies examined two ways of including the market price for risk: risk-adjusted discount rates and options-pricing methods.

The risk-adjusted discount rate (ADR) method "adds a spread—the difference between the interest rate on a Treasury security and the rate on a risky security—to Treasury rates and uses the resulting adjusted rate to discount expected cash flows associated with a loan."[71] The ADR method results in a higher discount rate for both costs and revenues and, with a few exceptions for negative subsidies, raises the net cost of credit programs.

An option is a contract that gives the buyer the right, but not the obligation, to buy or sell a specified quantity of an instrument at a specific price within a specified period of time, regardless of the market price of that instrument.[72] "The general idea behind options-pricing methods is that assets with the same payoffs must have the same price; otherwise, investors would have the opportunity to earn a risk-free profit by buying low and selling high."[73] An options-pricing method is likely to be more accurate than the ADR method but only when the necessary data and model are available.[74] Options-pricing models are seldom used to value credit provided to individuals; instead the use of the ADR method is usually appropriate.[75] Option-pricing methods are usually better than ADR methods in valuing credit provided to commercial enterprises.[76] The best method to use varies for other credit programs such as "loan assistance to sovereign states, municipalities, and special-purpose enterprises."[77]

As an example of the process, CBO applied a type of options pricing—the binomial pricing method—to calculate the risk-adjusted cost of extending federal loan guarantees to Chrysler in 1980 and to America West Airlines (AWA) in 2002. CBO computed that the market-value loss of the Chrysler loan guarantee was $239.0 million instead of the Treasury-rate loss of $107.6 million.[78] CBO also found that the calculated market-value loss was $26.3 million for the AWA loan guarantee instead of a gain of $47.4 million using Treasury interest rates.[79]

---

[70] Ibid., p. 3.

[71] Ibid., p. 7.

[72] For a detailed explanation of options, see CRS Report R40646, *Derivatives Regulation and Legislation Through the 111th Congress*, by Rena S. Miller, p. 27.

[73] Congressional Budget Office, *Estimating the Value of Subsidies for Federal Loans and Loan Guarantees*, August 2004, p. 8.

[74] Ibid.

[75] Ibid.

[76] Ibid.

[77] Ibid., p. 9.

[78] Ibid., pp. 12-19.

[79] Ibid.

In the President's budget for FY2013, the Office of Management and Budget selected "Fair Value Budgeting for Credit Programs" as a topic for in-depth analysis.[80] OMB compared and contrasted the current cost to the government with fair value budgeting. In March 2012, CBO released an issue brief titled *Fair-Value Accounting for Federal Credit Programs*.[81] CBO indicated its support for fair value accounting, but acknowledged that fair value accounting involves implementation issues.

CBO stated that "the government already uses fair-value estimates in budgeting for a few types of programs or transactions, including commitments of resources for some International Monetary Fund lending facilities and the Troubled Asset Relief Program."[82]

The weak economy and expansionary monetary policy caused low nominal Treasury interest rates from FY2009-FY2011. Consequently, the use of Treasury interest rates in the cost to the government measure resulted in aggregate costs of federal credit of negative $19 billion for FY2009, negative $20 billion for FY2010, and negative $41 billion for FY2011.[83] These negative costs reduced the sizes of the federal deficits. In contrast, the aggregate cost of federal credit averaged positive $3.1 billion annually for FY1998-FY2008.[84] Arguably, these negative aggregate costs of federal credit over the past three fiscal years have contributed to the debate about changing to fair value budgeting.[85]

Inclusion of Administrative Costs

As was discussed in the 1990 debate, administrative costs of credit programs could be included in the calculation of the costs of these programs. Proponents argue that the current exclusion of these costs understates the actual costs of credit programs. Proponents also stress that cost comparisons among credit programs are distorted. For example, the administrative costs per $1 million of credit are higher for direct student loans than guaranteed student loans. Opponents argue that agencies have difficulty separating the administrative costs of their credit programs from their general administrative costs.

In its analysis of fair-value budgeting, CBO stated,

> Comprehensive fair-value estimates of subsidies for credit programs would incorporate certain administrative expenses, such as servicing and collection costs, that are essential to preserving the value of the government's claims (rather than accounting separately for those costs on a cash basis). Those essential preservation expenses can differ significantly among credit programs, and including them in subsidy cost estimates would make comparing various subsidy costs easier. However, doing so could erode Congressional control over program expenditures because, under FCRA, all increases in estimated costs after a loan or loan guarantee is initiated (including those arising from increased expenditures on servicing

---

[80] U.S. Executive Office of the President, Office of Management and Budget, *Analytical Perspectives, Budget of the U.S. Government, Fiscal Year 2013* (Washington, DC: GPO. 2012), pp. 393-399.

[81] Congressional Budget Office, *Fair-Value Accounting for Federal Credit Programs*, March 2012.

[82] Ibid., p. 3.

[83] Congressional Budget Office, *Fair-Value Accounting for Federal Credit Programs*, p. 5.

[84] Ibid.

[85] For a comprehensive analysis of the debate over the inclusion of market risk, see CRS Report R42503, *Subsidy Cost of Federal Credit Cost to the Government or Fair Value Cost?*, by James M. Bickley.

or loan collection) are automatically appropriated. Another concern is that implementing a switch from cash to accrual accounting for essential preservation expenses would be administratively complicated.[86]

Proposed Legislation in the 112th Congress

Four bills have been introduced in the 112th Congress that include major proposals to reform the budgetary treatment of federal credit. Some of the reforms in these proposals were discussed extensively in the prior section of this report.[87]

S. 1651/H.R. 3414. Honest Budget Act

S. 1651 and H.R. 3414 are related bills. On October 4, 2011, Senator Jeff Sessions introduced S. 1651. On November 14, 2011, Representative Bill Huizenga introduced H.R. 3414.

The first purpose of these bills is identified as "to measure more accurately the costs of Federal credit programs by accounting for them on a fair value basis."[88] These bills define the term "cost" as "the sum of the Treasury discounting component and the risk component of a direct loan, loan guarantee, or financial investment or a modification thereof."[89] Beginning with FY2015, these bills expand the coverage of FCRA to include "financial investment programs."[90] These bills define the term financial investment as "an investment by the Government in any securities (debt or equity), stock, bonds, or futures, options, swaps, or other derivatives, issued by a non-federal entity…."[91]

These bills state that "all funding for an agency's administrative costs associated with a direct loan, loan guarantee, or financial investment program shall be displayed as distinct and separately identified subaccounts within the same budget account as the program's cost."[92]

H.R. 3581. Budget and Accounting Transparency Act of 2011

On December 7, 2011, Representative Scott Garrett introduced H.R. 3581. On February 7, 2012, the bill passed the House by a 245-180 vote.[93] On February 9, this act was referred to the Senate Committee on the Budget.

The first purpose identified in this bill is "to measure more accurately the costs of Federal Credit programs by accounting for them on a fair value basis."[94] This bill defines the term "cost" as "the

---

[86] Congressional Budget Office, *Fair-Value Accounting for Federal Credit* Programs, pp. 10-11.

[87] In addition, House Fiscal Year 2012 Budget Resolution (H.Con.Res. 34, 112th Congress) and House Fiscal Year 2013 Budget Resolution (H.Con Res. 112, 112th Congress) have provisions for the calculation of subsidy costs using fair value accounting.

[88] Section 501(1).

[89] Section 502(7)(A).

[90] Section 504(a).

[91] Section 502(5)(A).

[92] Section 504(g).

[93] For action by the House Budget Committee, see H.Rept. 112-380, Part 1.

---

sum of the Treasury discounting component and the risk component of a direct loan, loan guarantee, or financial investment or a modification thereof."[95] This bill states that

> Not later than 1 year after the date of enactment of this Act, the Directors of the Congressional Budget Office and the Office of Management and Budget shall each prepare a study and make recommendations to the Committees on the Budget of the House of Representatives and the Senate as to the feasibility of applying fair value concepts to budgeting for the costs of Federal insurance programs.[96]

This bill would require that the receipts and disbursements of the Federal National Mortgage Association (Fannie Mae) and the Federal Home Loan Mortgage Corporation (Freddie Mac) be included in the budget.[97] FCRA would thereby apply to these GSEs.

H.R. 3844. Honest Budget Act of 2012

On January 31, 2012, Representative Martha Roby introduced H.R. 3844. The sections concerning the budgetary treatment of federal credit are essentially the same as in the Honest Budget Act (S. 1651/H.R. 3414), which was described above.

(...continued)

[94] Section 501(1).

[95] Section 502(5)(A).

[96] Section 201.

[97] Section 202.

Appendix A. Concepts of Present Value and Future Value

The concepts of present value and future value can be explained by using simple examples.[98] A dollar received now is more valuable than a dollar received a year from now for the simple reason that if you have a dollar today, you can put it in the bank and have more than a dollar a year from now because of interest earning. Since dollars today are worth more than dollars in the future, we need some means of weighting cash flows that are received at different times in order that they can be compared. Mathematics provides us with the means of making such comparisons. With a few simple calculations, we can adjust the value of a dollar received any number of years from now in order that it can be compared with the value of a dollar in hand today.

The Mathematics of Interest:

The **future value** of an investment can be expressed in mathematical terms by means of the following formula or equation:

$$Fn = P(1+r)^n$$

Where: Fn = the balance (or future value) at the end of period n, P = the amount invested now, r = the rate of interest per period, and the n exponent is the number of periods.

Examples:

(1) Assume $100 is deposited in a bank saving account for one year, at an interest rate of 5%. Then $P = \$100$, $r = 0.05$, and $n = 1$. Under these conditions, the future value at the end of year 1 or $F1 = \$105$.

The $100 present outlay is called the present value of the $105 amount to be received in one year. It is also known as the discounted value of the future $105 receipt.

(2) Assume that the $105 is left in the bank for a second year at an interest rate of 5%. Thus, the initial $100 compounds over a two year period. Then $P = \$100$, $r = 0.05$, and $n = 2$. Under these conditions, the future value at the end of year 2 or $F2 = \$110.25$. Thus, at the end of the second year the original $100 deposit will have grown to $110.25.

The $100 present outlay is called the present value of the $110.25 amount to be received in two years. It is also know as the discounted value of the future $110.25 receipt.

The **present value** of any sum to be received in the future can be computed by turning the equation for future value or $Fn = P(1+r)^n$ around and solving for P: $P = Fn / (1+r)^n$.

---

[98] This appendix is an edited excerpt from the following website: http://www.accounting4management.com/ concept_of_present_value.htm.

Appendix B. Federal Credit Data

Table B-1. Estimated Future Cost of Outstanding Federal Credit Programs, FY2011

(in billions of dollars)

Program	Outstanding 2011	Estimated Future Costs of 2011 Outstanding[a]
Direct Loans:[b]		
Federal Student Loans	378	−14
GSE Mortgage-Backed Securities Purchase Program	71	−2
Troubled Asset Re ief Program[c]	100	42
Education Temporary Student Loan Purchase Authority	98	−13
Farm Service Agency (excl. CCC), Rural Development, Rural Housing	52	10
Rural Utilities Service and Rural Telephone Bank	47	2
State Housing Finance Authority Direct Loans	15	1
Disaster Assistance	8	2
Housing and Urban Development	9	7
Export-Import Bank	9	2
Public Law 480	5	2
Agency for International Development	4	1
Department of Energy, Title 17, ATVM	7	1
Small Business Lending Fund[c]	4	−*
Other direct loan programs[c]	31	11
Total direct loans	838	52
Guaranteed Loans:[b]		
FHA-Mutual Mortgage Insurance Fund	1,043	28
Federal Student Loans	328	10
Department of Veterans Affairs (VA) Mortgages	258	5
FHA-General and Special Risk Insurance Fund	138	8
Small Business Administration (SBA)[d]	82	5
Farm Service Agency (excl. CCC), Rural Development, Rural Housing	83	4
Export-Import Bank	49	1
International Assistance	20	3
Commodity Credit Corporation	6	*
Government National Mortgage Association (GNMA)	....	*
Other guaranteed loan programs[e]	10	1
Total guaranteed loans	2,017	64
Total Federal Credit	**2,855**	**116**

Source: Adapted by CRS from U.S. Executive Office of the President. Office of Management and Budget. *Analytical Perspectives, Budget of the United States Government, Fiscal Year 2013* (Washington: GPO, 2012), p. 401.

Notes: * = $500 mil ion or less.

a.   Direct loan future costs reflect the financing account allowance for subsidy cost and the liquidating account allowance for estimated uncollectible principal and interest. Loan guarantee future costs reflect estimated iabilities for loan guarantees

b.   Excludes loans and guarantees by deposit insurance agencies and programs not included under credit reform, such as Commodity Credit Corporation (CCC) commodity price supports. Defaulted guaranteed loans that result in loans receivable are included in direct loan amounts.

c.   As authorized by law, equity purchases under the TARP, the Small Business Lending Fund, and IMF Quota transactions provided in the Supplemental Appropriations Act of 2009 are included in the table. Future costs for TARP and IMF transactions reflected here are calculated using the discount rate required by the FCRA, adjusted for market risks, as directed in legislation.

d.   Certain SBA data are excluded from the totals because they are secondary guarantees on SBA's own guaranteed loans. GNMA guarantee data are excluded from the totals because they are secondary guarantees on loans guaranteed by FHA, VA and RHS.

e.   Includes Department of Energy Title 17 loan guarantees financed by private lenders.

Appendix C. Budgetary Treatment of Federal Credit Before FY1992

Before the implementation of the Federal Credit Reform Act of 1990, the unified budget treated federal credit in two different ways. The unified budget measured credit by its cash flows, but also, after 1980, included a separate credit budget that measured and selectively controlled gross credit flows.

Unified Budget

The federal unified budget used cash-basis accounting. Before FY1992, a new federal direct loan was treated as a budget outlay in the current fiscal year, and repayments of principal and payments of interest were treated as offsetting collections (negative outlays) in the future fiscal years in which they occurred. If a loan recipient paid a fee, this fee was treated as an offsetting collection. Loan defaults reduced repayments of principal and interest, and therefore offsetting collections. Administrative expenses were reported as outlays. In a given fiscal year, the budgetary cost of a loan program, not the individual loans, was its net cash flow. This equaled new loans made plus any administrative expenses associated with these loans (rarely recognized in the loan accounts) less any loan fees, repayments of principal, and payments of interest.

The federal acceptance of a contingent liability when a loan guarantee was provided was not included in the federal budget because no cash flow occurred. The administrative costs of a guarantee program were outlays in the fiscal year in which they occurred. Some guarantee programs charge fees to the recipient, and these fees were considered offsetting collections. Any federal outlays necessary to compensate lenders for any default losses covered by a federal guarantee were not shown in the budget until they were actually paid.

Credit Budget

In January 1980, the Office of Management and Budget introduced a federal "credit budget" to help monitor and control the growth of federal credit, including new direct loan obligations and new loan guarantee commitments. Federal credit was measured at the time that the government signed a binding contract to provide credit assistance. Initially, the credit budget consisted of nonbinding targets. Before FY1992, limits in the credit budget were included in the budget resolution and in annual appropriation acts for discretionary credit programs but not mandatory credit programs.[99] Although the credit budget improved credit visibility, the credit budget did not measure or control the size of subsidies.

The Federal Credit Reform Act of 1990 decreased the importance of the credit budget because control of credit subsidies largely replaced limits on gross credit flows as a determinant of the amount of new federal credit for each program. Estimated limitations on credit loan levels are proposed in each presidential budget, although the term "credit budget" is not used by OMB.[100]

---

[99] U.S. Executive Office of the President, Office of Management and Budget, *Special Analysis F, Federal Credit Programs, Budget of the United States Government, Fiscal Year 1990* (Washington, DC: GPO, 1989), p. F4.

[100] The estimated appropriation acts limitation on credit loan levels by program are published annually in the Analytical (continued...)

But these limitations on credit loan levels are set too high to realistically affect the amount of credit extended.

(...continued)
Perspectives, Budget of the United States.

Appendix D. Budgetary Treatment of a Hypothetical Direct Loan

(1) For a proposed direct loan program, CBO is required to estimate the subsidy cost if a bill including the loan program goes to the floor. If legislation is passed that includes a new loan program, OMB becomes responsible for estimating the subsidy cost. If a direct loan program "L" has been enacted into law, agency "A" establishes a credit program account and a nonbudget financing account.

(2) OMB in consultation with agency A estimates that the net present value of the cost of credit subsidies equals (in this example) 20% of loans disbursed under program L operated by agency A.

(3) If program L is a discretionary loan program, an appropriations bill for the fiscal year is passed by Congress and signed into law by the President.[101] This bill includes an appropriation of (in this example) $100 million for the subsidy budget authority of program L. Within agency A, this $100 million is appropriated to the credit program account for program L. Furthermore, this appropriations bill must include an estimate of the dollar amount of new direct loan obligations supportable by the subsidy budget authority appropriated to agency A for program L. For example, if program L has an estimated subsidy rate of 20%, the dollar amount of new direct loan obligations supportable would be $500 million.

(4) Agency A signs a contract to loan $10 million to a borrower under the auspices of program L. The estimated subsidy cost of this loan is $2 million (20% of $10 million).

(5) The borrower meets the terms and conditions of the loan contract. Agency A pays $2 million from its credit program account for L into its financing account for L. The financing account for program L borrows $8 million (unsubsidized portion of the loan) from the U.S. Treasury. At the same time that these budgetary transfers occur within agency A, the loan of $10 million is disbursed from the financing account for program L to the borrower. The subsidy payment of $2 million that goes into the financing account is scored as an outlay for agency A and for the federal budget. The $8 million borrowed from the Treasury is a non-budget means of financing, and consequently, does not affect the budget deficit, outlays, or revenues. But this $8 million, if the budget is in deficit, does increase the national debt.

(6) Agency A services the loan. Cash flows between the public and the non-budget financing account for fees, interest, defaults, etc., do not affect the budget deficit, outlays, or revenues. But the net cash flows of the financing account do affect the national debt.

(7) Repayments of principal and payments of interest are paid by the borrower into the financing account for program L. The financing account uses these monies to pay the interest and repay the principal on the $8 million borrowed from the Treasury.

---

[101] If program L is a mandatory loan program, an automatic appropriation of budget authority to cover the estimated subsidy costs would occur for whatever amount of credit is needed to meet the estimated demand for services by beneficiaries.

Appendix E. Budgetary Treatment of a Hypothetical Loan Guarantee

(1) For a proposed loan guarantee program, CBO would be required to estimate the subsidy cost if a bill including the loan guarantee program goes to the floor. If legislation is passed that includes a new loan guarantee program, OMB becomes responsible for estimating the subsidy cost. If a loan guarantee program "G" has been enacted into law, agency "A" establishes a credit program account and a financing account.

(2) OMB in consultation with agency A estimates that the net present value of the cost of credit subsidies equals (in this example) 10% of loans guaranteed under program G operated by agency A.

(3) If program G is a discretionary loan guarantee program, an appropriations bill for the fiscal year is passed by Congress and signed into law by the President.[102] This bill includes an appropriation (in this example) of $60 million for the subsidy budget authority for program G. Within agency A, this $60 million is placed in the credit program account for program G. Furthermore, this appropriations bill must include an estimate of the dollar amount of guaranteed loan commitments supportable by the subsidy budget authority appropriated to agency A for program G. For example, if program G has an estimated subsidy rate of 10%, the dollar amount of new guaranteed loan commitments supportable would be $600 million.

(4) Agency A signs a contract to guarantee a loan of $15 million to the borrower. The estimated subsidy cost of this guarantee is $1.5 million (10% of $15 million). The loan guarantee fee (if any) is paid by the borrower to the financing account for program G at the time the loan guarantee is obligated.

(5) After the borrower (lender, or other party to the agreement) meets the terms and conditions of the loan guarantee contract, the borrower obtains the loan from the lender in the private sector. Agency A pays $1.5 million from its credit program account for G into its financing account for G. At the same time that this budgetary transfer occurs within agency A, the agency provides the guarantee in order for the borrower to obtain the loan from the private lender. The subsidy payment of $1.5 million that goes into the financing account is scored as an outlay for agency A and for the federal budget. The borrower must pay to the lender interest on the principal and repay the principal.

(6) Agency A services the loan guarantee. The cash flows between the public and the non-budget financing account do not affect the budget deficit, outlays, or revenues. But the net cash flow from the financing account affects the national debt.

(7) The subsidy amount and any loan guarantee fee earn interest, which is paid by the Treasury. If the borrower defaults on all or part of the guaranteed loan then the financing account is responsible for covering the cost of compensating the lender.

---

[102] If program G is a mandatory loan guarantee program, an automatic appropriation of budget authority would occur for whatever amount of credit needed to meet the estimated demand for services by beneficiaries.

Appendix F. Direct Loan Data, FY2013

Table F-1. Subsidy Rates, Budget Authority, and Loan Levels for Proposed Direct Loans for FY2013

(in millions of dollars and percent)

Agency and Program	Subsidy Rate %	Subsidy Budget Authority $	Loan Levels $
Agriculture:			
Agricultural Credit Insurance Fund Program Account	4.80	77	1,632
Farm Storage Facility Loans Program Account	−2.47	−7	303
Rural Electrification and Telecommunications Loans Program Account	−5.55	−377	6,790
Distance Learning, Telemedicine, and Broadband Program	9.47	9	94
Rural Water and Waste Disposal Program Account	8.07	90	1,121
Rural Community Facilities Program Account	−2.08	−42	2,000
Farm Labor Program Account	....	....	....
Multifamily Housing Revitalization Program Account	60.20	31	51
Rural Housing Insurance Fund Program Account	7.28	52	707
Rural Microenterprise Investment Program Account	14.95	5	34
Rural Development Loan Fund Program Account	32.04	6	19
Rural Economic Development Loans Program Account	12.39	4	33
Commerce:			
Fisheries Finance Program Account	−4.21	−4	83
Defense—Military:			
Defense Family Housing Improvement Fund	....	....	....
Education:			
College Housing and Academic Facilities Loans	6.29	20	320
Teacher Education Assistance	10.89	11	97
Federal Perkins Loan Program Account	−29.10	−1,379	4,737
Federal Direct Student Loan Program Account	−20.08	−33,475	166,707
Energy:			
Title 17 Innovative Technology Loan Guarantee Program	.........[a]	....	15,000
Advanced Technology Vehicles Manufacturing Loan Program Account	....	....	....
Health and Human Services:			
Consumer Operated and Oriented Plan Program Account	43.05	699	1,625

Agency and Program	Subsidy Rate %	Subsidy Budget Authority $	Loan Levels $
Homeland Security:			
Disaster Assistance Direct Loan Program Account	−1.51	−1	25
Housing and Urban Development:			
FHA-Mutual Mortgage Insurance Program Account	....	....	50
FHA-General and Special Risk Program Account	....	....	1
Emergency Homeowners' Re ief Fund	....	....	....
State:			
Repatriation Loans Program Account	57.67	1	2
Transportation:			
TIFIA General Fund Program Account, Federal Highway Administration, Transportation	10.34	39	377
Federal-aid Highways	9.66	478	4,948
Railroad Rehabilitation and Improvement Program	....	....	600
Treasury:			
Small Business Lending Fund Program Account[b]	....	....	....
Community Development Financial Institutions Fund Program Account	0.78	8	1,025
Veterans Affairs:			
Veterans Housing Benefit Program Fund	−2.54	−33	1,326
Native American Veteran Housing Loan	−13.87	−2	14
International Assistance Programs:			
Development Credit Authority Program Account	....	34	....
Overseas Private Investment Corporation	−3.10	−36	1,150
Small Business Administration:			
Disaster Loans Program Account	11.11	122	1,100
Business Loans Program Account	15.71	3	18
Export-Import Bank of the United States:			
Export-Import Bank loans Program Account	30.08	8	25
National Infrastructure Bank:			
National Infrastructure Bank Program Account	15.02	338	2,250
Total	**N/A**	**−33,352**	**214,274**

Source: Adapted by CRS from U.S. Executive Office of the President. Office of Management and Budget, *Analytical Perspectives, Budget of the United States Government, Fiscal Year 2013* (Washington, DC: GPO, 2012), p. 405.

Notes: Additional information on credit subsidy rates is contained in the *Federal Credit Supplement* to the budget for 2013.

N/A = Not app icable.

a. Rate reflects notional estimate, including transactions funded through either appropriations or borrower fees. Estimates will be determined at the time of execution, and will reflect the terms of the contracts and other characteristics.

b. As authorized by law, equity purchases under the Small Business Lending Fund and IMF transactions provided in the Supplemental Appropriations Act of 2009 are included in the table.

Appendix G. Loan Guarantee Data, FY2013

**Table G-1. Subsidy Rates, Budget Authority, and Loan Levels for
Proposed Loan Guarantees for FY2013**

(in millions of dollars and percent)

Agency and Program	Subsidy Rate %	Subsidy Budget Authority $	Loan Levels $
Agriculture:			
Agriculture Credit Insurance Fund	0.52	17	3,150
Commodity Credit Corporation Export Loans	−0.81	−45	5,500
Rural Water and Waste Disposal Program Account	1.06	*	47
Rural Community Faci ities Program Account	6.75	1	16
Rural Housing Insurance Fund Program Account	−0.28	−67	24,150
Rural Business Program Account	6.86	67	981
Rural Energy for America Program	24.01	28	118
Commerce:			
Economic Development Assistance Programs	18.06	7	39
Energy:			
Title 17 Innovative Technology Loan Guarantee Program	....	....	....
Health and Human Services:			
Health Resources and Services	3.70	*	12
Housing and Urban Development:			
Indian Housing Loan Guarantee Fund	0.83	7	900
Native Hawaiian Housing Loan Guarantee	0.50	1	38
Native American Housing Block Grant	10.91	2	18
Community Development Loan Guarantees	....	....	500
FHA-Mutual Mortgage Insurance	−3.73	−8,188	219,562
FHA-General and Special Risk	−4.01	−661	16,435
Interior:			
Indian Guaranteed Loan Program Account	5.53	4	73
Transportation:			
Minority Business Resource Center Program	1.73	*	22
Federal-Aid Highways	9.50	20	211
Railroad Rehabilitation and Improvement Program	....	....	100
Maritime Guaranteed Loan (Title XI)	....	....	....
Veterans Affairs:			

Agency and Program	Subsidy Rate %	Subsidy Budget Authority $	Loan Levels $
Agriculture:			
Veterans Housing Benefit Program Fund	0.27	135	50,821
International Assistance Programs:			
Loan Guarantees to Israel Program Account	....	....	....
Development Credit Authority Program Account	6.45	47	729
Overseas Private Investment Corporation	−6.38	−185	2,900
Small Business Administration:			
Disaster Loans Program Account	2.31	1	57
Business Loans Program Account	0.45	374	83,440
Export-Import Bank of the United States:			
Export-Import Bank Loans Program Account	−2.83	−1,049	36,949
National Infrastructure Bank:			
National Infrastructure Bank Program Account	8.51	17	200
Total	**N/A**	**−9,467**	**446,968**
Addendum: Secondary Guaranteed Loan Commitments			
GNMA:			
Guarantees of Mortgage-backed Securities Loan Guarantee Program Account	−0.23	−550	239,000
Treasury:			
Troubled Asset Relief Program, Housing Programs[a]	4.76	2,466	51,862
SBA:			
Secondary Market Guarantee Program	....	....	12,000
Total, secondary guaranteed loan commitments	**N/A**	**1,916**	**302,862**

Source: Adapted by CRS from U.S. Executive Office of the President. Office of Management and Budget. *Analytical Perspectives, Budget of the United States Government, Fiscal Year 2013* (Washington, DC: GPO, 2012), p. 407.

Notes: Additional information on credit subsidy rates is contained in the Federal Credit Supplement.

N/A = Not applicable.

* = $500,000 or less.

a. Amounts reflect the TARP FHA Refinance Letter of Credit program. Subsidy costs for this program are calculated using the discount rate required by the FCRA, adjusted for market risks, as directed in legislation.

Author Contact Information

James M. Bickley
Specialist in Public Finance
jbickley@crs.loc.gov, 7-7794

www.ingramcontent.com/pod-product-compliance
Lightning Source LLC
Chambersburg PA
CBHW081409170526
45166CB00010B/3270